This book belongs to

_____

_____

To future investors—may your journey be magical!

Visit us on the web! www.econforkids.com

ISBN: 978-1-954945-25-8 (ebook)

ISBN: 978-1-954945-26-5 (paperback)

What Is a Stock?

By Kelly Lee

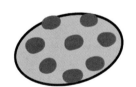

Econ for Kids

Charlie had a bakery that sold the best cookies and ice-cream sandwiches in town, but he had always dreamt of more.

"I want to make more yummy treats. I want to sell cakes, muffins, cupcakes, donuts, and more!" Charlie said to himself.

"I'm going to make the most amazing desserts ever," Charlie declared, his eyes sparkling with enthusiasm. He pictured himself as the dessert king of his town.

"It's time for a big change," Charlie decided. "I'll rename my shop Charlie's Dessert Kingdom and get a shiny new sign!"

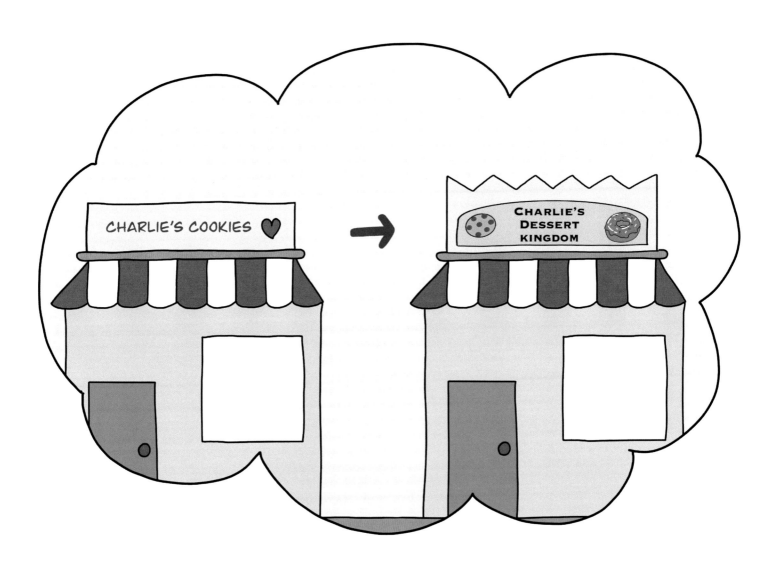

"I'll need a bigger oven, new baking tools, and additional ingredients," Charlie noted. The problem was, he needed money for all of this.

"It will cost $1000 in total," thought Charlie as he added up the price for each item.

TOOLS: $50

INGREDIENTS: $50

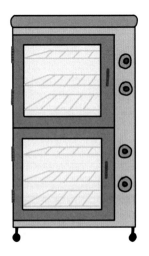

OVEN: $900

"I don't have enough money," Charlie sighed. "I could keep saving from selling my treats, but that could take a long time."

On a bright sunny day, Charlie had an amazing idea. He gathered his friends together to talk about how he could make the bakery better.

"Hi guys! I would like to create even more delicious treats, but I need some extra money. I have a plan that could help me raise money and also benefit my friends," Charlie announced with excitement.

"What's your plan, Charlie?" Hank asked.

Hank

Ava

Teddy

"It would involve my friends buying some shares of Charlie's Dessert Kingdom stock," Charlie answered. "Would you be interested?"

"What is a stock?" asked Ava, her eyes wide with curiosity.

"Imagine the bakery as a big cake," Charlie explained. "Buying a share of Charlie's Dessert Kingdom stock means you get a slice of the cake. Each share is like a piece of the bakery, and when you buy one, you become a part owner of the bakery!"

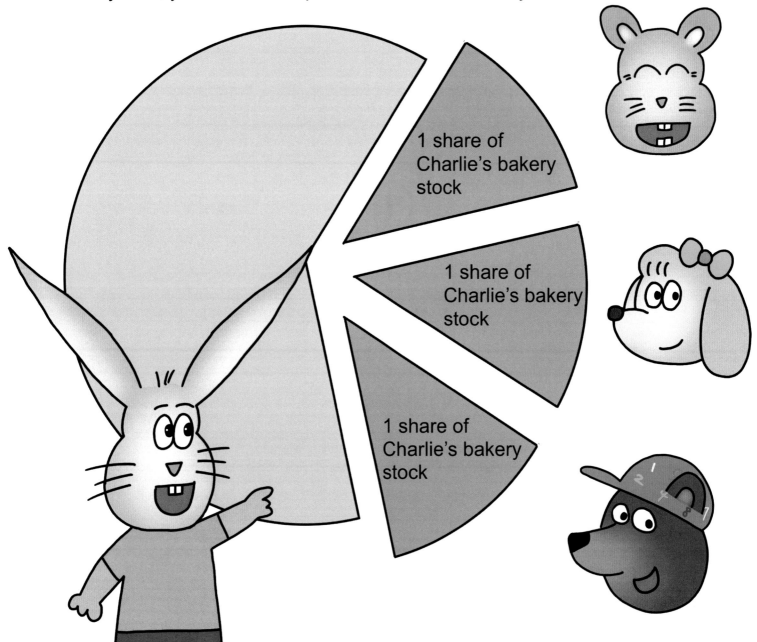

"What do we get for buying your stock?" Hank asked.

"The bakery will share a part of its profits with you," Charlie explained. "This money is called a dividend."

 Note: Profit is the money that Charlie earns after he pays for things such as the tools and ingredients needed to make desserts. Dividends are normally paid out once a quarter (every 3 months). Some companies pay dividends, and some don't.

"If Charlie's Dessert Kingdom becomes more valuable, so do your shares!" Charlie added. His friends looked puzzled.

When something is *valuable*, it means it's worth a lot. When a bakery makes lots of yummy treats and everyone loves them, it becomes more valuable.

"Imagine the bakery as a cake," Charlie continued. "When the bakery makes more money, the cake gets bigger, and so does your piece. That means your shares are worth more!"

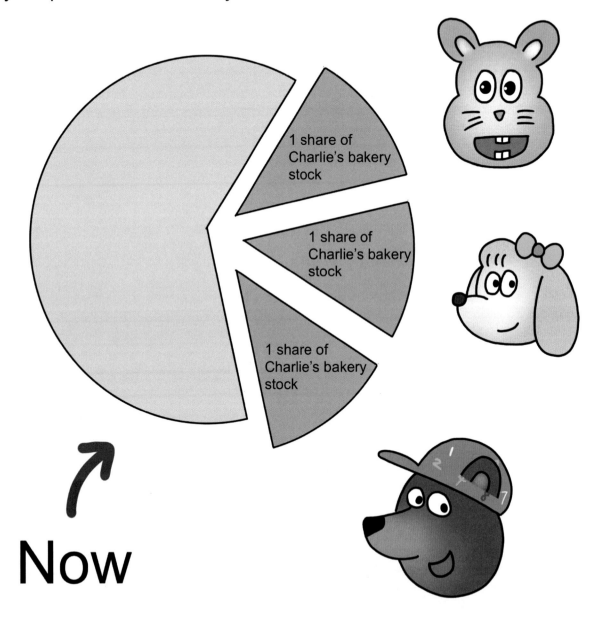

1 share of Charlie's bakery stock

1 share of Charlie's bakery stock

1 share of Charlie's bakery stock

Now

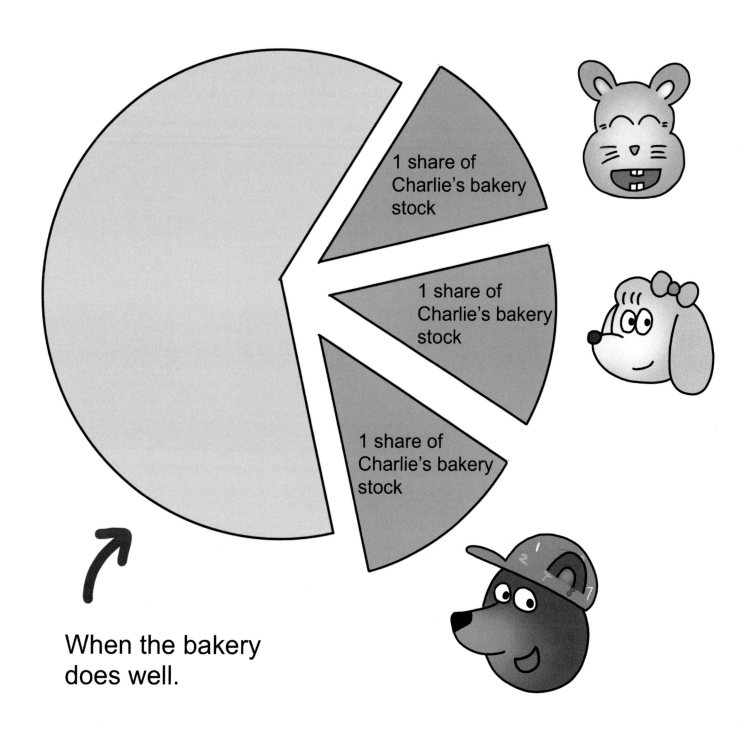

1 share of Charlie's bakery stock

1 share of Charlie's bakery stock

1 share of Charlie's bakery stock

When the bakery does well.

"Of course, if the bakery doesn't do well and loses money, the value of your shares could go down. But," he smiled confidently, "I'm pretty sure we are going to do awesome business!"

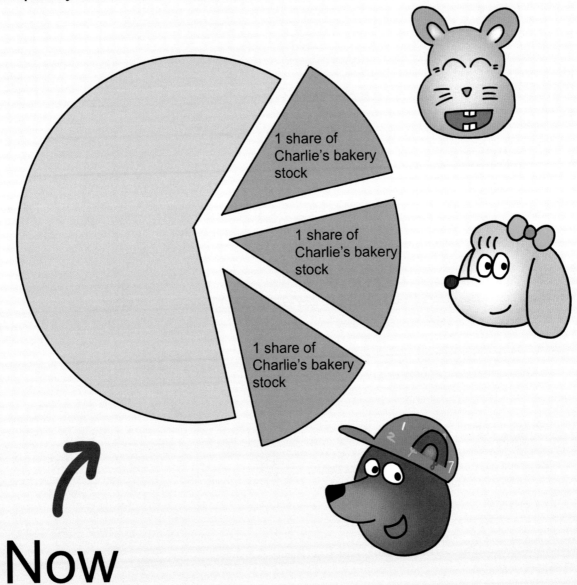

1 share of Charlie's bakery stock

1 share of Charlie's bakery stock

1 share of Charlie's bakery stock

Now

1 share of Charlie's bakery stock

1 share of Charlie's bakery stock

1 share of Charlie's bakery stock

When the bakery doesn't do well.

Hank, Ava, and Teddy were thrilled. They couldn't wait to make money and help Charlie's bakery grow. All of them decided to buy shares in Charlie's Dessert Kingdom.

Charlie got enough money to buy a shiny new oven, a bigger and brighter sign, and loads of ingredients for tasty treats.

The very next day, Charlie and his pals teamed up to give the bakery a fantastic makeover.

"Check out the most delicious desserts at Charlie's new bakery!" Teddy called out excitedly to passersby. They all put in a lot of effort to attract new customers.

Soon, the bakery became a favorite spot in town.

Charlie's Dessert Kingdom was a huge hit! A few months later, Charlie counted the money he had made.

"Thanks for believing in me and buying my bakery's stock," Charlie said with a big smile, as he handed each friend their dividend.

Together, Charlie and his friends discovered so much about running a business and the power of teamwork. They also got a real-life lesson on stocks and dividends.

Dear Parent/Grandparent/Caregiver,

Congratulations on giving your child a head start on their money-management journey! Stock is a complicated topic. Through a simple story, I'm hoping to highlight the following: 1) Buying shares of a stock means owning a piece of the company. 2) The value of a person's investment can rise or fall depending on how the company performs. The book aims to encourage your child to pay attention to the businesses around them, fostering an early awareness of the financial world.

Here are some fun activities you can do with your child to improve his or her understanding of stock:

- Look up any stock ticker symbol online. Explain to your child what company it represents and the cost of one share. Show them a historical chart of the stock to demonstrate how prices can change over time.

- When you are out and about, encourage your child to point out a shop they like. Ask questions such as "Why do you like this shop?" or "Would you buy part of their business?" The goal is to spark their curiosity and thinking—there are no wrong answers.

- Have them identify a shop that they don't like. Discuss it, ask questions such as "Why don't you like the shop?" or "Do you think it's not doing well as a business?"

- Consider setting up a meeting with a local business owner. This can give your child firsthand insight into running a business and its challenges. It's a great learning opportunity, even for younger children.

- Encourage your child to draw a picture of their ideal business and explain how it would work and make money. Ask them what would make it successful and what might not. This exercise is to foster creative and analytical thinking.

For clarification when sharing this story with your child, the question may arise whether "stock" is the same as "share." These terms are often used interchangeably but have subtle differences: "Stock" refers to general ownership in a company. Saying you own stock means you have a stake in one or more companies, but doesn't specify the quantity. "Share" is more specific. It represents a unit of stock. So owning shares means you have specific units of stock in a company.

For any questions, suggestions, or any other finance topics you would like to see in one of my books, please email kelly@econforkids.com. Thanks!

Kelly Lee

Little Economists Books

 What Is Money?

 What Is a Credit Card?

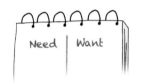 How to Spend Wisely

 What Is Supply and Demand?

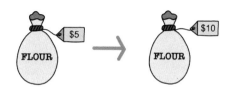 What Is Inflation?

And more!

Visit us at: www.econforkids.com

Made in the USA
Middletown, DE
13 October 2024

62547647R00020